NEW YORK REVIEW

POETS

ZUZANNA GIN[...]
and raised in Równe [...],
settled after fleeing from the violence of the Russian Civil
War. Both of her parents moved away from Równe while
Ginczanka was still a child—her father to the United States
to pursue an acting career, her mother to Spain with her new
husband—after which she was raised by her grandmother.
At eighteen, she moved to Warsaw and began publishing in
Szpilki and *Skamander* magazines, soon earning a reputation
as one of the most talented Polish poets of the interwar period.
Her friends included Witold Gombrowicz (who liked to play
pranks on her at his regular café) and Julian Tuwim (one of the
founders of the experimental literary group Skamander). Her
only volume of poetry, *On Centaurs*, appeared in 1936. When
Poland was invaded three years later, Ginczanka happened to
be visiting Równe, where Soviet forces soon seized her
grandmother's property. Ginczanka fled to Soviet-occupied
Lvov, where she married the art critic Michał Weinzieher and,
after the Nazi invasion of 1941, lived in hiding until 1943,
when her landlady denounced her to the authorities as a Jew
with false papers. Although Ginczanka was arrested, she
escaped and moved with Weinzieher to Kraków, where she
was arrested again and executed in 1944 or very early 1945,
shortly before the city was liberated by Soviet forces.

ALISSA VALLES is a poet and a lecturer in European
literature at Boston University; her translations from Polish
include Józef Czapski's *Memories of Starobielsk: Essays
Between Art and History* (NYRB Classics), Zbigniew Herbert's
Collected Poems and *Collected Prose*, and Ryszard Krynicki's
Our Life Grows (NYRB Poets).

Zuzanna Ginczanka

Firebird

TRANSLATED FROM THE POLISH
BY ALISSA VALLES

NYRB/POETS

 NEW YORK REVIEW BOOKS   *New York*

THIS IS A NEW YORK REVIEW BOOK
PUBLISHED BY THE NEW YORK REVIEW OF BOOKS
207 East 32nd Street, New York, NY 10016
www.nyrb.com

Library of Congress Cataloging-in-Publication Data
Names: Ginczanka, Zuzanna, 1917–1944, author. | Valles, Alissa, translator.
Title: Firebird / by Zuzanna Ginczanka; translated by Alissa Valles.
Description: New York: New York Review Books, [2023] | Series: New York
    Review Books poets | Includes bibliographical references.
Identifiers: LCCN 2022029609 (print) | LCCN 2022029610 (ebook) |
    ISBN 9781681377308 (paperback) | ISBN 9781681377315 (ebook)
Subjects: LCSH: Ginczanka, Zuzanna, 1917–1944—Translations into
    English. | LCGFT: Poetry.
Classification: LCC PG7158.G52 F57 2023 (print) | LCC PG7158.G52 (ebook)
    | DDC 891.8/517—dc23/eng/20220919
LC record available at https://lccn.loc.gov/2022029609
LC ebook record available at https://lccn.loc.gov/2022029610

ISBN 978-1-68137-730-8
Available as an electronic book; ISBN 978-1-68137-731-5

Cover and book design by Emily Singer

Printed in the United States of America on acid-free paper.
10 9 8 7 6 5 4 3 2 1

Contents

Non omnis moriar multaque pars mei
vitabit Libitinam
                    —Horace, Ode 3, 30

Non omnis moriar—my magnificent estate,
tablecloth meadows, steadfast fortress shelves,
my precious comforters and billowing sheets,
my dresses, my colorful dresses will survive.
I leave no heirs, so may your hand dig out
my Jewish things, Chominowa of Lvov, mother
of a Volksdeutscher, snitch's wife, swift snout.
May they serve you and yours, not any others.
My dears, this is no lute nor empty name,
I remember you, as you remembered me,
particularly when the Schupo came,
and carefully reminded them of me.
May my friends gather, sit and raise their glasses,
drink to my funeral and to their own rich gain—
carpets and tapestries, china, fine brasses—
drink throughout the night, and come the dawn

begin their mad hunt—under sofas and rugs,
in quilts and mattresses—for gems and gold.
O how the work will burn in their hands: plugs
of tangled horsehair and soft tufts of wool,
storms of burst pillows, clouds of goose down
will stick to their arms and turn them into wings;
my blood will seal the fresh feathers with oakum,
transforming birds of prey into sudden angels.

This untitled poem, written shortly before its author's ex-
ecution by the Gestapo in Kraków in 1944 or early 1945, has
come to occupy a curious position in the canon of Polish
literature. Zuzanna Ginczanka's last poem is, among other
things, a bitter parody of a classic Romantic lyric by the poet
Juliusz Słowacki. That lyric, "Testament mój," is imbued
with its own bitterness but asserts the Horatian triumph of
poetry over death with full confidence.

Who else would go without worldly accolades,
With such indifference to the world as I display?
As helmsman of a boat crowded full of shades,
Flying off as quiet as a shade when it flies away?

And yet I leave behind me this fateful power,
Useless while I live . . . it merely graces my temples;
But when I die, it will, unseen, press on you forever,
Till it remakes you, bread eaters—into angels.

Ginczanka's poem, hurled across time, both a testament
and a curse, strikes at the heart of the national myth built by

Słowacki and his contemporaries, who in the words of Czesław Miłosz cast Poland "as an innocent victim suffering for the sins of humanity." Ginczanka breaks cultural and poetic decorum by naming one person (though not the only one) responsible for her imminent death: a Polish woman concierge who denounced her to the Nazi occupation authorities as a Jew in hiding. In doing so, her parody reveals the reverse side of the coin of national pride and pious memory.

Instead of presenting her poems as her Horatian legacy, Ginczanka bestows her humble belongings in a rhetorical gesture on those she imagines, only too plausibly, to be looting her rooms after she is taken away by the Schutzpolizei. She preempts their theft—their grave-robbing—by giving her "Jewish things" away freely. It is an extraordinary instance of a poet who, facing death, finds the strength for a defiance of her fate and of national tradition. The poem hits home all the more forcefully at the present time because Poland is once again under the control of nationalists who use the dead cynically as pawns on the political chessboard: state propaganda elevates Polish rescuers and resisters, and the state criminalizes any public accusations of wartime collaboration and murder leveled at Poles.

Ginczanka's poem was rescued (accounts invariably say "miraculously"; certainly it was in very unlikely circumstances) and published in a Polish newspaper in 1946. Not long afterward, it featured in court proceedings against Pani Chominowa that resulted in a three-year prison sentence. (Her son, the "Volksdeutscher" mentioned in the poem, was also indicted but found innocent of collaboration.) Reprinted in a collection edited by Ginczanka's friend Jan Śpiewak in

1955, the poem and the poet then sank from view for decades, until the end of the communist era initiated a new surge in publications of banned or ignored writers. The 1990s brought a new edition of Ginczanka's poetry and a biography, as well as a new generation of feminist scholars who have seized on the power of her work, brief life, and—it must be said—beauty, to upend stale notions about the roles of poets, women, and Jews in Polish culture. She is now the focus of conferences, theses, exhibitions, anthologies, artists' commissions.

Ginczanka's life falls between those of Anna Świrszczyńska (b. 1909) and Wisława Szymborska (b. 1923), who share certain of her attributes—sexual frankness, caustic wit—but have a narrower emotional and formal range. Ginczanka combines a virtuoso sense of poetic form with barbed intellect and sensual exuberance, in accordance with the program laid out in her only book of poems, *On Centaurs*, a slender volume published in 1936, when she was a nineteen-year-old student at the University of Warsaw.

Any assessment of her work as a whole is shaped by the knowledge of her premature death, and it is a delicate business to distinguish real accomplishment from what were obviously awkward early experiments. In this respect she is like some of the English poets who died in World War I, whose later editors swayed between a sanctification of every scrap and a patronizing tendency to correct their youthful efforts. Just as Isaac Rosenberg's war poems were first published after his death in 1918 with conventionalizing editorial amendments, Ginczanka's "*Non omnis moriar*" was first printed with "corrections" by the influential poet and editor Julian Przyboś. Her early poems had been seized on and promoted by Julian Tuwim, the doyen of Warsaw poets, who encouraged Ginczanka to come to the capital from the borderland town of Równe, now Rivne in Ukraine. From the start, these poems tended to reverse traditional accounts of the relation of body to spirit, and to mock hypocrisy about sex and social identity. In this they are a bit reminiscent of the odd, bold poems of Mina Loy, herself a figure who sank into obscurity after a glamorous youth and was rediscovered decades later (fortunately, in her case, while she was still alive).

There is deep melancholy in many of Ginczanka's poems, but no lamentation. She is neither patient nor meek and, in every gesture, rejects the view that moral progress is made through suffering and endurance. She is not particularly interested in morality nor in progress, whether public or private. She is interested in life, and her negations serve it, stripping away the surface glamour of the modernist interbellum and the underlying deposits of Romantic sentiment that was erupting as political fanaticism on the right and left in the 1930s. Ginczanka, consumed in the war's storm of destruction, is and remains a poet of anticipation—she looks ahead fearlessly to love, knowledge, joy, and ultimately doom. Much of her poetry takes place in the future tense; she escaped commemoration as a poet's task.

Ginczanka is a poet of the vocative case, even when addressing dead things. She calls them out for their scandalous lack of life:

> O lynxes, wildcats, pumas stuffed with fluff,
> foxes with yellow linings and yellow glass eyes,
> O far-flung fleece, splayed flat and crafty,

far-flung mornings
pinned fast on dreams,
O quaggy wolfish woody needles, hair of fir trees,
chaos of bear's bristle,
muddle of troubled days—
—I brush you with sharp scorn,
O fur of my windblown springtimes,
loose shaggy fur
without flesh
bone
or blood.

("Fur")

Libitina, the goddess of funerals and burials, has a passionate cult in Poland, but one that is fraught with ambiguity. In his magisterial "cultural history of mortal remains," *The Work of the Dead*, Thomas Laqueur describes in rich detail the tendency of certain cultures to attach complex meaning and value to dwelling near the dead, what he calls "necrosociability." The aura of relics and remains has historically increased the prestige of certain geographical areas, much as today the value of real estate may be boosted by proximity to the sea or to a high-end shopping street. Słowacki in his testament takes heart from the knowledge that his friends will have his remains in their care. Laqueur's book traces a shift from this traditional taste for living in neighborly congregation with the departed to a twentieth-century preoccupation with the names of the dead, and particularly those who, in the words of Zbigniew Herbert, "are given the bizarre name / of the lost," those specters for whom we have no remains but whose death is nonetheless a certainty. To this modern obsession—for it is clearly more than a fashion—Laqueur gives the strange name of "necronominalism." Poland is a country where, for reasons that are only too obvious, the necro-sociability of an overwhelmingly Catholic culture and the necronominalism related to the vast numbers of lost and unburied dead, predominantly Jewish, continually compete and clash with each other in painful and public ways.

The mortal remains of Polish poets have been subject to an unusual degree of turbulence. When Adam Mickiewicz, the towering figure of Romantic poetry, died in 1855, he was in Constantinople on a diplomatic mission for the French during the Crimean War. His body was shipped to Paris for burial at Montmorency cemetery, then in 1890 his remains were returned to Poland and reinterred at the Wawel Royal Castle in Kraków. Similarly, the slightly younger Słowacki, who died of tuberculosis in Paris in 1849 and was initially buried at Montmartre, was dug up and "translated" to the fatherland in 1927 and deposited in the Wawel crypt in a grand ceremony; the presence of the head of state of independent Poland, Józef Piłsudski, elevated the occasion to the level of a major political event. The third of the "national bards," Zygmunt Krasiński, died in Paris in 1859, and his remains were brought back to Poland to be buried in the graveyard of his family's estate at Opinogóra, where there is now fittingly a Museum of Romanticism.

In 2017, on the occasion of the centennial of her birth in Kiev as Zuzanna Gincburg, Ginczanka formally entered the ranks of the Polish dead: A memorial plaque for her was unveiled on the wall of the building where she had last lived in hiding, on Szpitalna Street in Kraków. It does not mention a Polish denouncer, just the Germans who led her from the house to prison and death. But during an arts festival in Lublin in 2020, a performance artist caused a scandal with an installation displayed in a street near the former ghetto: a sign spelling out the name CHOMINOWA in yellow neon. The act of provocation was abhorred by many, including the Ginczanka scholar Izolda Kiec, but the artist, who once drew a mustache on Poland's most sacred icon, the Black Madonna of Częstochowa, seems to have hit a nerve. The sign appears to have released currents of shame and guilt over the history of collaboration, along with countercurrents of anger and outrage at the suggestion that a Polish *szmalcownik*, or collaborator, could be worthy of public memory, all compounded by the cheap promotional gimmicks associated with neon. You want to dream of Polish heroes, it seemed to say: I'll light up your nightmares with the name of a Polish hag.

The line engraved on Ginczanka's plaque is from the poem "On Centaurs": "I call for passion and wisdom / joined at the waist / like a centaur." With the phrase "poet of the Polish language by choice," the inscription points to her preferring Polish over the other borderland languages she could have selected as her medium. Russian was the language she spoke with the grandmother who brought her up after her parents had emigrated: it is pliable in texture, exuberant and incantatory in rhythm; Yiddish would have put her squarely in the center of an international modernist movement which boasted many powerful female voices and could have won her readers in New York, Buenos Aires, and Tel Aviv. No: She chose Polish, a language that as Aleksander Wat remarked (in an essay titled "The Translatability of Poetic Works"), is harsh and rough, more suitable as material for sculpture than for painting. She has become part of the language, but it is not a resting place for her. Although she wrote under a pseudonym, it is as Jewish as her birth name. She evaded Libitina in the sense that she had no burial, but Horace uses the goddess's name as a metonym for death. Hers was a Jewish death, and her *"non omnis moriar"* cannot be—as it is in Horace, or Pushkin, or Słowacki—a joyful gesture of self-giving. Słowacki in his "Testament" testifies that he suffered with his fellow Poles and derives from this the right to call them to future sacrifice; he imagines for his own poems a role in creating a spiritual home for them. Ginczanka knows that the monument she is erecting to herself can only be a painful reminder of the failure of her compatriots to suffer with her. To do so—to receive her gift—they would have to relegate their dream of Poland to the Museum of Romanticism.

I raise my visor sleepily and go, conscious of my losses, into the still, frozen underground, full of subterranean memories and dreams wafting from walls. Exhaustion crushes my throat, and I trail a harsh wake of poems.

(from "Firebird")

—*Alissa Valles*

ACKNOWLEDGMENTS

For clues, criticism, support, and scholarship, I give warm thanks to Agata Araszkiewicz, Sarmen Beglarian, Anna Bikont, Monika Fabijańska, Victoria Frede-Montemayor, Irena Grudzińska Gross, Sharon Grosso, Bożena Keff, Masza Potocka, and Maggie Vlietstra.

Every reader of Zuzanna Ginczanka is deeply indebted to professor Izolda Kiec, whose passionate research and editorial work has made this poet available in exquisite form. I have based all translations in this book on the text as established in Kiec's 2019 edition *Poezje zebrane* (1931–1944).

Work on this book was supported in part by the Beatrice Bain Research Group, University of California, Berkeley, in 2022, and by a grant from the National Endowment for the Arts in 2018.

On Centaurs (1936)

On Centaurs

Whetting rhyme on rhyme, sharpening verse lines grind
—don't trust calculations, lest they ensnare your mind
—don't trust your fingers like the blind,
nor your eyes like owls without hands—
I call for passion and wisdom
joined at the waist
like a centaur.—

I profess the proud harmony of a man's head and torso
with a stallion's hefty body and slender fetlock—
magnificent centaurs gallop
toward cool cheeks of women
and the round withers of mares
amid horseshoes ringing from meadows of myth.

Their curbed and wise passion
and their wisdom fiery as bliss
I found in proud harmony
and fused at waist and heart.

Look:
thought
with its ancient face
trusted its divinity to steaming horses,
like tethered steeds in a buttercup field
the quivering senses dash across June.

Process

1.

In the beginning were heaven and earth:
black lipids and oxygen, cornflower blue—
and fawns
alongside sinuous deer
with a god soft and white as linen.

2.

O Cretaceous,
Jurassic,
Triassic,
the soil splits into strata—
the Miocene charges, a tank in imperial conquest.
And there is division of the water
from the earth of birch and fern
—and god sees that it is good when genesis rises at dawn.
Nitrogen infuses in lava,
lava freezes like varnish,
mountain
climbs
mountain
in a thundering cosmic straddling,
carbon saturates the earth with petrified coal pulp—
—and he sees that it is good for the stars and moist
    amphibians.
Iron pulses bloodily,
phosphor hardens in tibia—
—and he whistles in the pipes of craters like a singing breeze.

3.

In the beginning were heaven and earth
and fawns
and tawny deer.
And then the course changes:
behold
flesh
became
word.

4.

Once under a fragrant angel a splendid rhododendron
    trembled,
horsetails scratched and scraped as big and tall as New York.
In Konin, Brest, and Równe
daisies wither
in the squares
and at night
policemen
make love
to wedded
wives.

Pride

Thick-veined flaxen-haired maidens meet wholemeal youths,
fresh-breathed angels present their astral bodies.
I know:
I'm entangled in good and evil
as in the hundredfold three-leafedness of clover—
Mixed in bast baskets the apples of all knowledge rattle.

> So I'm meant to ask the way
> to You,
> lost as I am on the crossroads of dreams?
> So many times day has blackened blue eyes with
>   black night—
> Eighteen faded Junes
> screaming
> won't hear
> the question—
> Eighteen winters won't hear gray winters dumb as a
>   stump.

Women's warm leaf-tongues rub and scatter words on the
    wind—
a fanatical aluminum snake weaves a nest in the paradise
    tree.
I don't know, Lord,
what's good,
what's evil,
fixed on my eighteen years—
rapt stern and alert
more and more
wiser and wiser
I don't know.

Canticum canticorum

The fruits of the vineyard foam,
　　　Sweet-smelling spikenard
　　　　　Wafts across the gardens
I pastured my brothers' flock
　　　In the heat of the sun—
　　　　　That is why I am black.
The blue night thunders,
　　　The yellow stars burn
　　　　　The heavens turn to ash.
I hide my glowing eyes
　　　In my lashes' cypress grove
　　　　　As in the pools of Hazebon.

"O my love, open to me—
　　　I've run through the garden—
　　　　　A wispy rose in my curls—
Repeat your lips to me
　　　That I may wonder again
　　　　　If you tasted apple tonight"—
"How can I open to you
　　　the creaking doors—
　　　　　when I've undone my dress
Mothers will thrice curse me
　　　And the flock of goats
　　　　　Will give no sweet milk."

The blue night thunders
　　　And the vine plants are blasted
　　　　　And the leaves of the fig trees—
And I can't sleep at all,
　　　I open the wooden gate—

But my love has gone.
Fragrance of saffron and cassia.
The oil has run over,
Myrrh on the door latch.
The path slowly vanishes
Like an unraveled stitch,
Black-eyed dark by the porch.

I sought but didn't find him.
My voice called out to him
But he offered no reply.
(He, handsome as a star,
As the depths of the heavens—
Anyone will know him.)
I call you fragrant maidens
By the deer of the forest
By the doe quick as a sign:
Do not seek love before time
Do not strive to rouse it
Till it come to you on its own.

Matter

A weighty thick Pacific whirrs under its sheet of glass
a rosy-fleshed panther bursts from its silky fur—
the biblical whale of God spills its burning oil,
like God's biblical archangel doused stars in splendor.

You see—
that's just why.
Black earth splits the pavement.
Under every silent layer you can scent matter erupting.
The sky is singed by stars
as if by blown-out torches—
the ebb and flow of trains announces the surging of time.

And when you shout:
"laugh,"
thirty-two-toothed womenfolk whinny.
And when you whisper:
"death,"
a deaf-mute
blindness
stifles.
Trembling animals strain, those you lured from the wild,
those whose names you uttered
whom you glorified with names.

Warm red things are born from phrases as from mothers
matter bursts in a gush of blood from lyrical anguish.
A name buds with world—
world swells with beyond—
and you
pronounce

words grown flesh
like the Creator—
in terror.—

Embezzlement

O days of ruble and thaler, clanging,
June rang with chervontsi,
rang a jangling purse—
a moon-gleam polished
midnights
like tails of coins—
sun dazzled the gleanings
with noons
like two-headed eagles—

—and I myself, and I weak
with chimeras
forgot that these days were
yours.

Navigation

In the tar-sealed ark of my overheated affairs
I flee
the flood's lashing frenzy
and the whistling world—
I led gentle doves out of the distant storm of phenomena,
amphibians out of gleaming mica
and splendid bendy worms.

Symbols with cosmic wings
and lacquered claws
cling to the tawny manes of beasts from the biblical ark.
O torpor's dull elephants rocking dreams on your brows!
O pride, O eagle's talons dug ecstatic into necks of lions!

The world strikes the vessel in a vicious metallic wave—
—there
     a dark
         release
             of chaos
a hostile furious flood—
—how many days before slender-waisted apple trees
with their pink bows begin to shimmer in the valleys?—
Here it smells of resin,
the essence of colors freezes,
a wiry soprano of Marches winds around July's alto.
In the tar-sealed ark of my overheated affairs
I flee
the flood's lashing frenzy
and the whistling world.

Fur

O lynxes, wildcats, pumas stuffed with fluff,
foxes with yellow linings and yellow glass eyes,
O far-flung fleece, splayed flat and crafty,
far-flung mornings
pinned fast on dreams,
O quaggy wolfish woody needles, hair of fir trees,
chaos of bear's bristle,
muddle of troubled days—
I brush you with sharp scorn,
O fur of my windblown springtimes,
loose shaggy fur
without flesh
bone
or blood.

Grammar

(—and taking root in words is such delight,
and it's so easy to fall in love with words—
just take them in hand to study like a burgundy under the
    light.)

Adjectives stretch out like cats
and like cats are made for caresses
soft cats warm and zaftig purr a tender andante and maesto.
Soft cats' eyes are lakes with drowned weeds in their depths
I gaze sleepily into a cat's pupils
mysterious glassy and *treacherous.*

Here is mass and form, here is irrevocable substance,
concrete essence of things, matter forged into a noun,
and world's stillness, dead things' peace and permanence,
the thing that endures and is, word contracted into body.
Here are simple *tables* and hard wooden *benches,*
here are frail wet *grasses* made of vegetable tissue,
here is the red-brick *church* that puts the Gothic into God
and here with its veins and arteries the simplest human
    heart.

Whereas adverbs are a sudden miracle
an astonishment of worn flint
there was something I don't know how—
but now it is *thoroughly through and through*
and embraces thought *two-fistedly* and is *surely* and
    wistfully and *well.*

And pronouns are tiny little rooms
where flowerpots grow in windows.

Each corner a memento of the past
and they're only for *you* and for *me*.
Here in an enigmatic abracadabra
the laws of love's algebra blossom:
I am *you, you* are *I* (comparison)
I without you—you without me is zero.
At dusk we like to grope around
little words like dresser drawers.
I am you, you are I. Comparison.
But pronouns are secret as flowers
like the tiniest tiny little rooms,
where you live hidden from the world.

(—so just take a word into your hand,
study it like a burgundy under light,
taking root in words is such delight,
it's so easy to fall in love with them.—)

Virginity

We...
A rain-spattered thicket of hazel
fragrant with a rich pulp of nuts;
cows are calving in the sultry air
in barns that burn like the stars.—
O black currants and guzzling grain
gathering juices to overflowing,
O she-wolves nursing their cubs,
she-wolves' eyes sweet as lilies!
The honey-hive resin trickles,
the goat's melon udder swings—
—white milk flows like eternity
in the temples of mothers' breasts.

And we...
...hermetically sealed
as steel thermoses
in cubicles
of peach wallpaper
swathed in throat-high dresses
conduct
cultural
conversations.

The One Thing

Days flung like boomerangs return as sharp-tipped
    reminders:
gorgeous maidens were simpering,
woolly sheep came down from the mountains—
—what drove you on through it all—consider, calculate
    clearly,
what drove you on through the song—
the singing forest—
the wooden song—
the grove—

O watercolor mornings, greasy oils of noon,
sleepy pastels of evening and coal of deepest nights!
The stable pails drew bliss from a sharp source—
this drove you on,
this,
through fluttering, flags and ribbons.

This now drives you through tenderness:
(—cargo ships sail
laden with blessed Madonnas with skin made of touch
    and wax,
maidens full of sweetness, tender and smiling,
have faces scented with primrose and hair of ruddy
    nasturtiums.)

This drives you on through pathos:
(—the pedestals of victories cool.
Your hand flies upward. The banner flies up over your hand.
Lightning stupefies the apple tree's root. Life comes
    crashing down.

And delight dazes like a fragrance. Bird cherry throbs at
    your temple.)

In a mute arctic past you wander with the maps of
    memories—
O never-filling pails,
bottomless tin pails!
You drew a sharp spring's bliss from every source.
I consider, calculate, and know:
this is the one thing
that drives you.

Betrayal

No one can watch over me.
The sin of suede and bats
hangs in terror's attic with its mousy head down—
At dawn I'll escape the tower, I'll flee the watchtower
through a sharp wasps' slit
through a tangle of poisoned weeds—

From the rubble will rise the crushing crags of
commandments
the Vedas' twenty hells,
flames,
howls,
and whistling,
the fanatical night will threaten, petrify with its stars,
like mercury I'll slip through your fingers.
Nothing can watch over me.

You'll change into a wolf, I a wagtail—
you an eagle, I a devious sprite—
with inscrutable wit I'll thwart your every hunter's ploy.
The world can't watch over me,
O favorite—O dear—O lovely,
if I myself
don't choose
sweet May's
fidelity.

Explanation in the Margin

I did not rise
from dust,
I will not turn
to dust.
I did not descend
from heaven
and I won't return
to heaven.
I myself am heaven,
like a glass vault.
I myself am earth,
like fertile clay.
I haven't fled
from anywhere
nor will I return
there.
I know no remove but myself.
In the wind's swelling lung
and in calcifying rock
I must
find myself
as I am
scattered
here.

Otherness

Look:
A purple troubadour festoons the day with trumpets—
the merchants distribute scarlet and sulfurous balm—
singing girls sway, melting on soprano glass stilts—
and dancers' torsos and ankles jingle with trinkets—
but you have worn yourself thin
in these streets
you walk
every day,
and in you, death is sure
as a needle that swims in your veins.

Joy sails by
in the distance
in a festive pink boat
down a far foreign river
made of ultramarine and silt.
They will say of your grief: "a flatfoot midget"
they will say of your sorrow: "egg white, roses, and oil."
Neither sheer cambric lyrics
nor an epic heavy as brocade
will reveal you
to anyone
in a hint from beyond the seven seas.

Declaration

THESIS

Rough-tongued animals came to know true taste—
Amorous hungry wolves full of sage experience.
Here is the present moment:
Insects gnaw at it in the elderblossom,
wasps with sharp stings drilled into the sweet dregs.
The earth turns on a spit—fragrant roasted venison.
The sun burns its mark like erythema's resinous flame.
O banquet of carnivores!
With the sharp sense of immemorial hungers
animals with rough tongues came to know true taste.

ANTITHESIS

People, their muscles atrophied, know aftertaste and
    foretaste.
Aftertaste—old men's history.
Foretaste—glow of prophets.
And the inner taste of the nucleus pulposus, warm and
    acrid cherry,
and the plum soft with juice, all grow far beyond the
    window.
(History: "O springtime of nations, O uprising like wildfire,
O year 1848, resounding and unforgotten!"
Prophecy: "O springtime of colonies, spring flowering on
    the seas,
in '48 you'll arrive as the ravaging of Africas!")
They nest in chamois leather,

in the bear's soft furs,
they know
that it was—
that it will be—
but today: an empty eye socket.
Today the daily half-moon toils in the cloudy milk
and tables grow in cafés like stumps in withered gardens.

SYNTHESIS

I know the seesaw foretaste
aftertaste's boundless quiet
and I caress the moment with my mouth
when it awakens
warm from sleep.
I'm nothing but a sagacious sort of animal
and nothing but a sharp-sensed sort of human.

Instead of a Rose Petal

My tiny city has a few too many streets
(I count them all daily, yet we never meet).
My tiny city has a couple of streets too few—
(but not one for a meeting of just us two).

My tiny city could stand above a thousand
of the sort whose sidewalks run on and on
and each with millions of slender dwellings,
people crawling ant-like like pits in melons,—
—each different everyday filled by your love
could ring the bells of meetings over the roof,
over houses like a giant piano's colored keys
—and we would walk
without end
and in us there'd be peace.

My tiny city could stand on a short mini street
just the one and only, as narrow as a creek,
and that little street could have just two houses
facing each other, laughing bells to rouse us—
we could go out from our houses in the evening
or in the morning: laughing, joyful, springlike,
and meet right there, hand-in-hand hearts ringing
and gaze into each other's eyes
without end
without end
as long as we both would live.

My tiny city has too few mini streets
and a few tiny streets in excess
of what I could guess...

Catch

FISHERWOMAN
I drove eyes like safety pins sharply into the world—
a ray shot yellow spun like a drill in my eyes—
suddenly like a fiery disk
brightness fell, reflected in a pupil—
suddenly in the blink of an eyelid
the world slipped from my eye's grip.
I ensnare a bay of phenomena
in the fishnets of my senses—
look:
a pale slippery fish is a pale slippery day—
the crunch of gravel, seed, and cinder
reveals things in hints—
I cast the nets and say:
"what I know,
what I know,
that I know."—

SEA
I poured myself out wide, profuse as an epic
in the green song of leaves,
in the red song of the blood—
believe in me
believe sight unseen
believe blindly as you do in the epic,
as you do in the epic of pale-fleshed silver-shelled days—
I spilled life from the spruces with a cut in the tarry bark
I—
the spluttering sea—a world frothing with song.
And you—
fisherwoman on the shore

you compose an elaborate aphorism
because your mouth,
your fingers,
your ears
catch only the wind—

FISHERWOMAN
I cast the nets and say:
"what I know,
what I know,
that I know"—
I know the taste the flesh of an apple leaves on the lips—
cherries sleepy as mouths droop down from sleepy trees—
a pear tree split into two hearts
bears the sign of juice flowing.

SEA
(The earth goes to law with God, its voice hoarse from
    tremors,
lava rumbles, curses the earth in thunder and roar—)
Fisherwoman of the other shore, in vain you cast your nets:
for the fish you can't see
at the frothing shoreline—
on shore you speak of nets
tie five senses with bindweed
but you don't know how much you lack to sail out to fish—
        How does the moon smell on ice?
        How does the seabed taste?
        How can your patchy and narrow senses
        grasp
        flocks
        of angels?

FISHERWOMAN

I just know of cinder and gravel
that they grate—
of a wave splashing like scales
that it teems—
of a blackbird gleaming in grass
that it's sated—
and of the lips' shimmer and song
that it's a dream.

Uncollected Poems (1936–1944)

Hearing

GIRL

Barometers pulse with mercury. Epochs' waves break on
  granite.
Cinnabar-tinted isobar lines slither through a zone of cut
  grass.
Faithful wives cinched at the waist, ready for women's
  business
anoint themselves with rich scents and don immodest
  velvet.
Midnight melts the burned-out red of the West into silver
  oxide.
Nervous sensitive antennae circle in somnambulist rows.
I sing splendid resounding events, a full-blown botanical
  Eden,
tops of things bursting with blossoms, wild manes of
  gardens.

TRIBUNAL

You miss what's essential for things to blossom *en rose*,
don't hiss: "The lion lies in wait on the road and the sword."
Harrow the dense earth, there's something woven beneath it,
look for the sucking roots under the mosses of misty
  ravines.
You roll around dully, lazy, on the froth of downy bed-
  clothes
when you have so long a road ahead and it can't be cut
  short;
before a world born of hydrogen returns to natural hydrogen,
you have still to travel across great and quarrelsome
  history.

GIRL

Don't pass sentence on me. The tide is foaming with
   dreams,
my hands are still unaccustomed to swimming across the
   sea,
I look, still sleepy and weak: epochs' waves break on granite,
the rolling waves of epochs carry the flotsam of lonely
   barks.

TRIBUNAL

Good Amon, tender Osiris,
the salt of Cain's sons hardened in your bones,
burned into resistant phosphors,
the skeleton lines itself with exact spans—
Yellow Amon, a good-natured god
ordered you to swim against the tide;
you are the stuff of quarrelsome history,
you are the world's only contents.
Swim then from life to life,
leave signs and words
how in wavy entanglements
to contend with a blunt wave.

GIRL

Nights hum like shells, biblical bushes burn,
the noble grave Joanna shears sheep's wool.
O starry waymarkers, signs unfathomed in time,
forebodings left unattended, full of rousing reminders!
O glass lodestars, with polar deer antlers,
signs given to me which I don't know how to read!
Foolish, I squandered in the buzz of a glorious noon

the nightly hoofbeat of bird cherry through ruined gates.
Don't pass sentence on me. More signs will confound me
before I find the roots of things that moss hides underfoot,
before I leave off the roar of events, the full-blown botanical
    Eden,
tops of things bursting with blossoms and the windblown
    manes of gardens.

Flight

Incandescent with color, the wild garden stands in earth
    like a wick,
touch a red burning like a flame and earth will go off like
    fireworks—
a proud peacock of rainbow enamel struts in the full light
    of the sun
beyond the lane of leafy maples planted in a long green row.

So it is by day: floating sunflowers, sparks of sharp
    crowfeet sown,
the leaves of the maple covered in varnish, and majestic
    peacocks;
midnight bright as yellow noon with the sheen and shine
    of lightning,
thunderclap after thunderclap lights up the trees with
    shine and sheen alone.

I wander the lonely rooms, thinking of an unknown garden,
staring at gray wallpaper, listening rapt to scratch and swish,
I—the only known earth amid the dead planets in orbit,
amid things of blatant color and of obscure, unclear
    essence—

I look in mirrors' standing pools and swim up like a
    drowned man,
I probe my eyes with a frightened hand and feel the hard
    socket,
then—a cry—and I run blindly out to the peacock-bright
    garden,
to the bronze burning trees and the elder tree burned to
    white,

I fall into the trembling of chestnuts, into the swaying of
    hazel and willow,
the bustle of turbid appearance and secret, murky essence—
I weep for pity,
I kiss your mouth,
I burst out laughing
and knit my brow,
I've nothing but life left in life
to forget stone-cold about death.

Contemporary

Look at the smashed decks, look at the helpless crew:
scientists wacky as crabs, fixed ecstatically on radium,
a youth with a banner who just now swayed and fell,
prophets foretelling earth from flimsy sinking ships,

poets gone silent from the cold, as the icy unchosen age
from an eternity set with stars hit and robbed them again,
from flimsy sinking ships they saw shores as if in a palm:
there, the greenery is fresh and the spring's water sweet.

And look at the other crowd, the ship cocky in its ropes,
a vat holding robust wine went off with a bang like a shell,
an old man strokes a curly beard, threatens cold planetary
    fires,
and Odoacer, chieftain of the Herulians, roars a fiery oration,

squealing, temple prostitutes hurl a fluttering flock of
    laughs
to the black eagles of curses, to wasted faces of zealous
    monks.
Here birdlike and noisy you scorn the dark stertorous
    flights,
entangled in drunk confusion, in the piercing, pulsing
    laughter.

Now you know ships will perish, perfidious seawalls break,
and the cocky ship will sink without seeing the tender shore
where spring water is sweet and the grass so fragrant and
    new,
and where milk and honey flows.

                                    So I confide in you our hopes.

Firebird

I don't know my fulfillment as I don't know my death.
Amid what sandalwood trees and among what angels,
bracing its vocal cords with the tongue's wise sting
does Firebird with flaming feathers call and disquiet?

Under a zoological sky the breathless animal park
marries a lion's star sign with an ardent live lioness;
I run through lovers' groves. The earth stirs to flight,
the sky slowly falls. They will meet at my lips.
Will a wing strike me here and dazzle my eyes with light,
where June, burning rose of winds, budded and bloomed?
I run, alert, and look: in the grass, girlish girdles
and sharp-shooting bows of hunters in another lost chase.
My love saw and chose me—and here he strides like a
      lion:
"A ship sails today, to tenderness, it waits with raised
      banner!"
In vain. I know: I will not go. Not yet here, not now
will the birdsong smother my breath like molten lead.
For there's a flapping of wings. Dreams' flutter and fright.
A feather lost in flight tickles the soft moon.
In the distance a protracted gurgle. The call. And again
I don't know my fulfillment as I don't know my death.

The chase leads me from green lovers' groves into battle,
the Firebird with its feathers unfurled circles over the field,
commanders check their armor, scenting honor and glory,
I cover my face with a visor in mind of knightly customs,
and draw my heavy sword—my eye circling upwards.
My indomitable chief races, scattering enemies with his
      voice:

"A ship departs for victory, it waits with resonant
    banner!"
In vain. I know I won't go. Firebird plunged me in a cloud.

I raise my visor sleepily and go, conscious of my losses,
into the still, frozen underground, full of subterranean
memories and dreams wafting from walls. Exhaustion
crushes my throat, and I trail a harsh wake of poems.
In quarries of sorrow I disavow birds and fulfillments,
I touch a column of basalt; "Lord," I repeat, singing—
"try me with grief, despair, the pit of ruin and death
but don't try me with happiness; I won't stand the test."

But suddenly—a flap of flight. I think I hear a far voice,
I run back into the green moist grassland, and again,
bracing vocal cords with the tongue's wise sting,
Firebird with flaming feathers calls and disquiets.
But there is no absolute thing—and therefore no thing
can cast me into ultimate love, or ultimate doubt or rage,
the feathers' flash can't scare me, nor the song calm me,
nor will the wing strike me or throw me backward.

Vocations

Praising the craft of war in poems slashed by the censor,
with violent rhyme and valiant hatred of man for man,
youngsters with thighs of flint tightly bound in leather
went with a clang of greaves and terrible flash of arms.

Euphorbus stabbed Patroclus; beautifully Hector gored him,
Hector was beautifully slain by thunder-helmeted Achilles!
Sing the club and ax, the brave and double-edged blade,
the arduous dance of blows, keen foresight of resistance.

Yours is the task of judging in a forceful soldierly stanza
man's hatred for man, and clothing the verdict in a chant—
while my fiery task
is to strain in the night's cool pitchers
the resonant honey
of a woman's
different
song.

Return

The waterfalls are raged out. A peaceful current flows in
with a wide wave of placations. A cloud freezes at dawn.
The invisible spheres of faraway planets revolve,
bees gather warm and liquid nectar from stems.

Where is this brightness from? From over there. A scent
of young forest, a stream of radiance revolves and rustles,
and in giant forest bounds sixteen-year-old witches
look for fledglings fallen from their nests in the night.

Into the forest comes Minerva, goddess of ripe wisdom
that flows from experience, she who brings harmony,
casts a tranquil eye on the raged-out waters,
adjusts a bouquet of violets from Olympus on her robe,
and says:

"Cast a patterned veil over secret things,
so the outline of hidden meanings can't be seen.
Be reconciled to appearances. Bind yourself to the world
not by tiresome reasoning but by quickening love.
Hasten your return to old truths, and celebrate it
to the sound of trumpets, a loud rustle of ribbons,
horns, drums, and flutes. Enough to call evil, evil,
and you know what to avoid, the orchestra's din nears.
Return to the tender embrace of warm family love,
to hands grasped long in fine tenacious friendship,
to pious and humble thoughts, cheering amusements,
to tireless labor in the service of a worthy end.
Finally, don't look for the great love of a man:
there are no visible signs by which to know it.

Choose a brave young man, make him a promise,
and a quick flame will leap from fiery lips to heart."

Gentle landscapes poured out like lakes,
streams springing from dreams filled up the ravines.
Sail on them. It's a return with a flag wrapped on the mast,
for a thing that I missed or came to notice too late—

and here, mindful of warnings, I see and see around me
things full of harmony, lights, magnificent forms,
and noble proportion. No storm comes near,
the wave is flat as glass. And it won't burst. This is peace.

Libra

How do you know love? By the inner commotion?
When you stumble on an arm's downward curve
seven times finer than others? By the winged dress
you embroider with thread and weave with flowers
to be gorgeous and worthy of a flame in the eye?
Or by the faithful habit of steps that melt together
and breathe in harmony and the hand that finds
an always ready hand when it longs for a touch?
Or the relief felt on returning from the fray
to a face as to a homeland when the ships sail in
after a faraway journey? Or is it by the cry when
betrayal hits, the tearing away and the falling back,
tearing away again, crying out, body weakening
like a dove pierced by a feathered arrow flutters?

How do you know love? Joined in a tight embrace
they stand, each disquieted by a body too close by,
searching silently for signs. You will see two statues
unmoving under a sailing cloud, on the water, where
two trout chase a cloud's reflection or, dusk to dawn,
pursue the sign of Capricorn, Leo, Pisces, and Aries.
An embrace joined them under a cloud, on the water.
By what law? Reflected in the rushing stream, slowly
they weigh the matter. Eyes in eyes, eyes in mouth,
mouth in mouth. How then to know it, by what?
Is it by the winged dress, by the winged dress
you embroider with thread and weave with flowers?
One takes Libra now from stream, now from sky,
saying mournfully: by the fact you don't need a sign.

Trophy

The dark-haired one flashed an amulet on a wristband,
the fair-haired one clicked beads of precious jasper,
and one had fragrant ornaments of choicest sandalwood,
who enticed me with a famous ring from foreign lands
who promised smooth-shaped amber, caressing my hand.

I'll come to you and boast tenderly:
"Here is my neck,
bare,
and my hands unadorned with ornament."

Sacrilege

Unbeknownst to you I dodged the shining statues
garlanded with shells and flashing tiger's teeth
and onward past the idols made of polished ivory
and the others cast in hollow silver and gold.
What can you do to me for wandering stubbornly,
seeking the heaviest doors and the hairiest turns?

Until in the dark sanctuary whose guard I fooled
I stood before
your stone despair
face
to Face.

Landscapes (fragments)

The poet dresses in silk and fastens his curly hair
with a star extinct in the galaxy;
at the gates open to the east the horses now stir
for a fast-harnessed temporality.

He quit sleepless nights and pain. Thereby he quit
song that flows from that pain.
Night slammed shut, pain ceased, song fell silent,
and the horses tug at their reins.

Prophets like trombonists swelled with horn-mad rage,
stony on wreaths of cloud:
"Saved be the song with wings of strumming plumage
that died a moment ago."

Handsome in a ruff and jabot the poet breaks the key
to the night that he has quit,
and rides in a light carriage into gardens of faded feasts,
fragrant avenues of delights,

where palm fronds growing from the stems of open hands
entwined with ivy the velvet
from where kittenish women predisposed to erotic favors
fish for him with their eyelids.

There rolls the wagonette. Birds of gold and glitter
have nested in her coats of arms
during graceful bows, courtly adieux and meetings
on the crossroads of promenades.

—What will this road be like, what images on the road
on which the poet sets out?
It will be these images and a road like this. In the East,
wind and sand and drought.

◆ ◆ ◆

An oarsman pushed off a boat and the wave approaching
soaked him, bringing out the hidden shape of his thigh—
When the burning wind struck, it made folds in his clothes.
That wind struck at dawn and warmed the shore till dusk,
till the sea became stormy and began to come to a boil,
scalding reefs of coral. That was the beginning of things.

And conquering the indolence native to northern seas
with a wave drawn out on shore like a dead frozen tongue,
boiling blue mercury broke from its tether
and crept across land like a turtle under the veil of night—
ships lay wrecked on the deserted seabed
with shattered hulls and lopped-off masts.

Ships with masts intact went with the streaming sea,
finding a dock at times on the peak of a rocky mountain,
or winding into valleys, making their way to the meadows
where insects were rubbing their legs against shiny wings—
and after leaving the mountains and sailing out of the
    valleys
the ships sailed across the open sea to capital cities,

the capitals of expansive states. In each capital and city
poets fell silent waiting for the wave to arrive.
They tuned their harps, replacing the ram's gut strings
with copper strings to announce to the cities melodiously

the moment the wave would roll in. Strings shone at night
like mute lightning flashes just ahead of the thunder.

And when the sea came in, above the deep blue depths
ships got caught on the roofs of town halls and towers—
Later capitals like islands lost to human memory
pressed from within, pushed up and out,
began to emerge once again. The sea swam on.
The poets seized their harps and sang history.

How the oarsman pushed off, how the approaching wave
soaked him, revealing the hidden shape of his thigh,
how the hot wind hit at dawn and warmed the shore till
    dusk.
But handsome in ruff and jabot, the poet didn't sing the
    abyss
in the gardens of faded feasts. That first song was taken
    away.

◆　◆　◆

Blind and trustful to a fault you rush into current time,
deceived by the ease of the road which aids your steps,
but I know time will condemn you
and therein lies my advantage, though your fist is hostile
and angry and there's a haughty gleam in your eye.

Here you lost your craft and strength,
and if you don't grasp the sign you won't recall the warning,
the sky with fiery crosses,
a terrible enemy graveyard
on the shell of exploded mountains foretells your later fate.

Then the landscape will change. As if at the call of a flute
the rats of fading memories will crawl out of cellars and
    attics.
You'll fall, stricken by fear
and secretly, quietly
they will bore through your heart to your silver bones.

So you confess with pain and shame: a hate with eagle's
    claws
had its hold on me in those days. And the shame will save
    your name,
for if you don't fall, crushed,
the cool face of history will look on your hate
from under the arch of its stone brow.

1938

Banquet (fragment of the poem "Landscapes")

BANQUETERS
Let us sit down at the table, gentlemen! But let the poet
who joins us for refreshment leave the place of honor free.
The orchestra is tuning, trumpets, harp, piccolos, and zither,
soon the flute will sound and choirs open the feast.
Let us sit down at the table, gentlemen! When the flute
    sounds
let each take his place in accordance with seniority and
    service.

FIRST CHOIR
Things lie far apart, and a sharp sword divides them,
so each thing stands alone. How to give them order?
All the ferries are burned, all the bridges are in ruins,
event obliterates event, grass overgrows their tracks.
You'll be true to nothing, multiplicity will overcome you.
Winged and swift horses will find you in tender arms.

SECOND CHOIR
Truly there's nothing but embraces and bewitchments,
event melts into event, body passes into body.
So where is that other thing if you cannot see the cuts
that mark the edges deep. Everything is the same thing.
You'll betray nothing, unity will always overcome you.
Tender arms will lift you from the swift-winged horses.

BANQUETERS
May that mature man come, may a mature man come,
whom we can respect for the virtues of his intellect,
who has eloquent lips, speech like the flesh of a fruit,
but whose bitter dry word rectifies a muddled matter.
We've waited too long for him at our banquet table,
let him come to us here and reject one song or the other.

POET, APPROACHING
Both songs are beautiful, filled with sublime tones,
plaintive zithers, tender harps, and festive horns,
both find in me the same kind of grateful listener,
standing on the song's bankside, why go in deep?
O clear color of the clarinet, low rumble of drums,
no one will fight through your tone, reach the truth.

BANQUETERS
Trembling we waited for the man and called him thrice,
until, late, he came at last. But does our ear delude us?
His tongue is crooked, his speech is rife with lies,
because the truth is one between revelations of two.
A hungry two-stinged worm sucked words from within.
So we reject them in silence
and turn away our eyes.

Epitaph

...And when through a dark wood the dark valley swam,
slipping over turtles, sinking into tall anthills,
jumping into surging streams, falling on moss, I chased
your elusive smile, shining out in a murky haze.

...Nothing was left of your face. Nothing—just features set
in a face open to the eye, bare bones of your former face.
Fleeting clouds of associations, as if scattered by winds,
fell from your features as from cliffs so that I'd see them now.

...So that is your smile! Blue frigates of memory,
pink frigates of daydreams, covered it with their sails
spread for flight. So that's your forehead! Your temples!
Mouth! Love's image masked your mouth until now.

May 1939

Sometimes I'm filled with hope
sometimes I'm troubled by fear.
Too much is going on—
It will come: either love or war.

There are signs it will be war:
a comet, speeches, orations.
There are signs it will be love:
the heart and palpitations.

A night-time comet flashed,
the dailies came from afar.
O springtime, spring of love!
No, not of love. Of war!

The height of spring has come
carrying dreams from above.
O springtime, spring of war!
No, not of war. Of love!

I read the daily updates,
spinning conclusions wildly.
I tear the petals off daisies:
he loves—likes—admires me...

Promising! Hostile! O spring
different from other springs!
I'll accept and endure it all,
whatever it is you bring.

I stand on the crossroads of May
where paths collide and scatter,
but both these springtime ways
must lead to ultimate matters.

Clouds of longing float in
and news sails down the wire.
Will I win out in the end
or will my ending be dire?

Awakening

The world—unknowable thicket, collage of images—
flickered with questions. There, in the red glare
of fires that never cease why do the warriors
reach again and again for a solid victory?
Why do folk, floating down the maze of streets,
grow hot with anger and gather like a flood tide?
Why does a shrouded and fitful reality come
with sorrow and dread and without maidenhood
or dowry to deliver nothing into longing arms?
Who won't betray us now, who won't spurn us?
The past, full of misadventure, is unfathomable.
Prophets wielding the power of a secret charm
led docile peoples out from captivity, parting
the waters on their way with a divining rod.
The future, in a veil of mist, cannot be seen.
What is the effort of our creation good for,
if nothing will follow? Press a palm to your brow.
Why do fern fronds spread streaks of seeds
by burning anthills, by the tracks of an animal?
Is it true that one and two-headed eagles armed
with swords and losing scraps of feather in flight
flutter out from state seals on a hunt for prey?
And amid the stars, blinking its stiff eyelashes
sits the eye of Providence. Or maybe it's a spider?

Here I watch, awoken from nightmares and visions.
From the chaos that jostles mists and mysteries
a great and simple world emerges in the mind,
magnetic metals, lush plants, heroic feats.
O matter, varied in your manifestations, who fill
and instill every thing and every cause with pith!

Above a cloud a light bird lifts its tail like a rudder
and warms a feather. I know—you're the bird,
the cloud and the solar flame. If a master stuns
with immortal work you flash in his mind and dig
into his heart. And if people raise angry faces
against another cloud with a contrary pressure,
you cut through the air with a spark of revolution.
(From a sharp clash will spill a lightning motion.)
And I can feel you inside me, O intimate matter,
you who ally me to birds, to the mass of clouds.
Reconciled with all I make my songs for friends
and they bring cotton flowers to busy workshops
for me. We embrace. Before us we can see
a sea full of coral reefs, behind us—history.
Whenever we listen to the past that lies behind us,
the gunshots whirr, a smooth stone rattles,
an iron plow and steel needles grind,
a gear belt booms. From these ordinary things
grows the tree of history. And now in the distance
the green sea filled with red coral
lies under the armored ships, hostile to us.
Before the ships complete the course they began
they'll change their flags to ours. Past and future
merge and continuity links all fires together.
O the gladness that flows from knowable things!
O rapid rivers of albumen! O mounds of carbon!
O sweetness of cognition! Darkness falls, fades.
Delicate mica gleams, streams run white,
and slender trees grow in open country.
I watch the stars. I see. And I burn with delight.

Battle for the Harvest

When the battle's over and the shells grow cold
you celebrate victory in epics and white marble.
Here too, battles rage. Sudden spring dawns
show you the space waxing like a furnace glow,
show you the space of the fields of beetroot.
Praise it with gleaming and thrumming string.

Deep under a hard leaf juicy vegetables
burgeon with life as sweet as your blood,
when a shield suddenly cracks, black armor rattles,
an honest beetle crawls up and rubs itself.
Pierced flesh dries, rust covers the leaves.
To arms! It's the enemy, come for the harvest!

Where will relief come from? Swift and cruel
may it strike the enemy—battle knows no mercy.
Such radiance is in the furious eyes of girls
when with festive braids swinging they lead
gentle silver hens with the softest feathers,
carrying relief to the fields and future bounty.

The beak pecks like a bayonet, turning the tide
of battle. The braid and feathers endure in granite.
May the poem's fiery caesura give them praise;
let the song recount to summers yet to come
how a rough hoarse pathos rose in these fields
amid vegetable greenery and created new days.

Non omnis moriar—my magnificent estate,
tablecloth meadows, steadfast fortress shelves,
my precious comforters and billowing sheets,
my dresses, my colorful dresses will survive.
I leave no heirs, so may your hand dig out
my Jewish things, Chominowa of Lvov, mother
of a Volksdeutscher, snitch's wife, swift snout.
May they serve you and yours, not any others.
My dears, this is no lute nor empty name,
I remember you, as you remembered me,
particularly when the Schupo came,
and carefully reminded them of me.
May my friends gather, sit and raise their glasses,
drink to my funeral and to their own rich gain—
carpets and tapestries, china, fine brasses—
drink throughout the night, and come the dawn
begin their mad hunt—under sofas and rugs,
in quilts and mattresses—for gems and gold.
O how the work will burn in their hands: plugs
of tangled horsehair and soft tufts of wool,
storms of burst pillows, clouds of goose down
will stick to their arms and turn them into wings;
my blood will seal the fresh feathers with oakum,
transforming birds of prey into sudden angels.